Make a Money Chart

My money chart
I want to buy
It costs
I have
I need to save
Ways to get money

a skateboard
$50
$20
$30
save my pocket money

do more jobs at home

help Grandpa wash his car

By Julie Haydon

Photographs by Lyz Turner-Clark

Goal

To make a money chart.

My money chart	
I want to buy	a skateboard
It costs	$50
I have	$20
I need to save	$30
Ways to get money	save my pocket money
	do more jobs at home
	help Grandpa wash his car

Materials

You will need:

- paper
- a pencil
- a ruler.

Steps

1. Rule a line down the middle of the paper to make a chart.

2. Write these words on the **left** side of the chart:

My money chart

I want to buy

It costs

My money chart
I want to buy
It costs

3. Write what you want to buy on the **right** side of the chart.

4. Write how much it will cost.

My money chart	
I want to buy	a skateboard
It costs	$50

5. Write these words on the **left** side of the chart:

I have

I need to save

My money chart	
I want to buy	a skateboard
It costs	$50
I have	
I need to save	

6. Write how much money you have now on the **right** side of the chart.

7. Write how much money you need to save.

My money chart	
I want to buy	a skateboard
It costs	$50
I have	$20
I need to save	$30

8. Write these words on the **left** side of the chart:

Ways to get money

9. Write the ways you will get money on the **right** side of the chart.

My money chart	
I want to buy	a skateboard
It costs	$50
I have	$20
I need to save	$30
Ways to get money	save my pocket money
	do more jobs at home
	help Grandpa wash his car

10. Save your money.

My money chart

I want to buy	a skateboard
It costs	$50
I have	$20
I need to save	$30
Ways to get money	save my pocket money
	do more jobs at home
	help Grandpa wash his car